2011 GREATEST Pop & MOVIE Hits

Arranged by Dan Coates

W9-AUF-645

CONTENTS

Billionaire (Travie McCoy featuring Bruno Mars) 2

Born This Way (Lady Gaga) 7

Born to Be Somebody (from *Never Say Never*).......12

Dream Is Collapsing (from *Inception*) 16

Firework (Katy Perry) 20

Forget You (Cee Lo Green)........................25

Grenade (Bruno Mars) 30

Haven't Met You Yet (Michael Bublé)......................35

Jar of Hearts (Christina Perri)....................40

Just the Way You Are (Amazing) (Bruno Mars).........50

Not Like the Movies (Katy Perry)............................45

Obliviate (from *Harry Potter and the Deathly Hallows, Part 1*) 58

You Haven't Seen the Last of Me (from *Burlesque*) 54

THE BIGGEST MOVIES ★ THE GREATEST ARTISTS

Alfred

Produced by
Alfred Music Publishing Co., Inc.
P.O. Box 10003
Van Nuys, CA 91410-0003
alfred.com

Printed in USA.

ISBN-10: 0-7390-8274-4
ISBN-13: 978-0-7390-8274-4

 Alfred Cares. Contents printed on 100% recycled paper.

BILLIONAIRE

Words and Music by
Peter Hernandez, Philip Lawrence,
Ari Levine and Travis McCoy
Arranged by Dan Coates

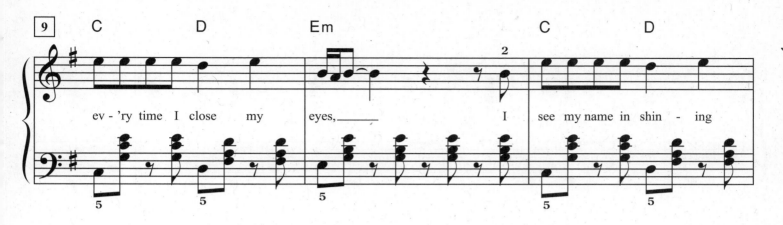

ev-'ry time I close my eyes,_____ I see my name in shin - ing

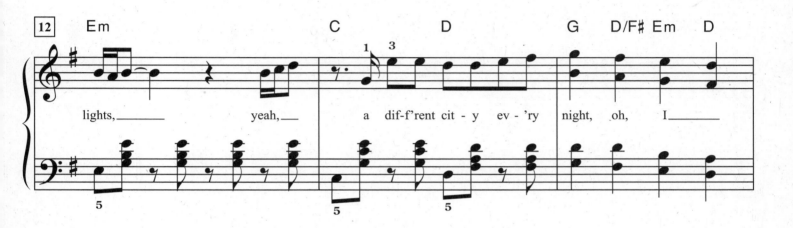

lights,_____ yeah,___ a dif-f'rent cit - y ev - 'ry night, oh, I_____

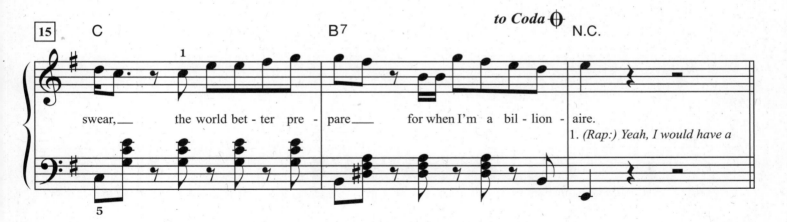

to Coda ⊕

swear,___ the world bet - ter pre - pare___ for when I'm a bil - lion - aire.

1. (Rap:) Yeah, I would have a

Verse:

show like Oprah. I would be the host of   *everyday Christmas. Give Travie a wish list.*

4

Bridge:

ev - 'ry time I close my eyes, I see my name in shin - ing

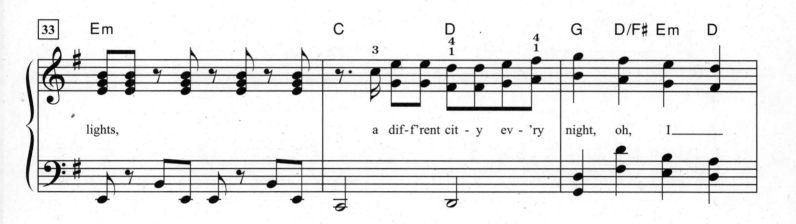

lights, a dif-f'rent cit - y ev - 'ry night, oh, I_____

swear,____ the world bet - ter pre - pare____ for when I'm a bil - lion -

aire. Oh,_____ oh,_____ when I'm a bil - lion - aire. Oh,_____ oh.

6

Verse 2:
(Rap)
I'll be playing basketball with the President
Dunking on his delegates,
Then I'll compliment him on his political etiquette,
Toss a couple milli in the air just for the heck of it,
But keep the fives, twenties, tens, and Bens completely separate.
Yeah, I'll be in a whole new tax bracket.
We in a recession, but let me take a crack at it.
I'll probably take whatever's left and just split it up,
So everybody that I love can have a couple bucks.
And not a single tummy around me
Would know what hungry was, eating good, sleeping soundly.
I know we all have a similar dream.
Go in your pocket, pull out your wallet, put it in the air and sing.

BORN THIS WAY

Words and Music by
Fernando Garibay, Stefani Germanotta,
Jeppe Laursen and Paul Blair
Arranged by Dan Coates

Moderate dance beat

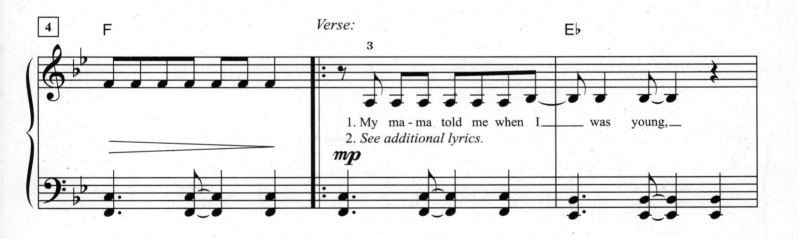

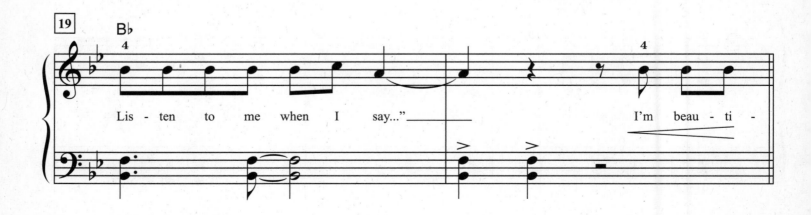

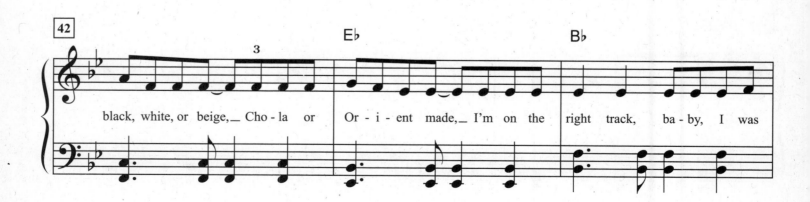

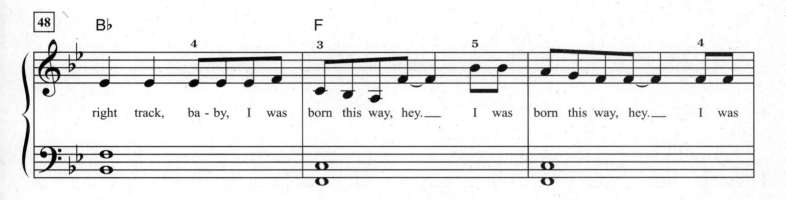

Verse 2:
Give yourself prudence, and love your friends.
Subway kid, rejoice your truth.
In the religion of the insecure,
I must be myself, respect my youth.
A different lover is not a sin.
Believe capital H.I.M.
I love my life, I love this record and,
Mi amore vole fe ya. *(Same DNA.)*
(To Chorus:)

BORN TO BE SOMEBODY

Words and Music by Diane Warren
Arranged by Dan Coates

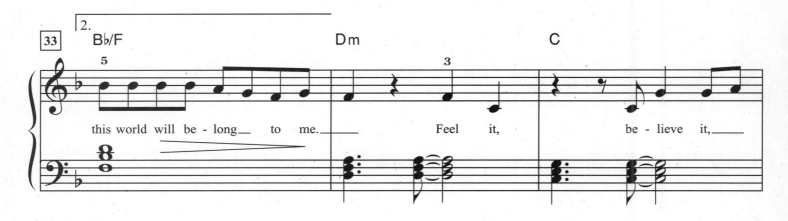

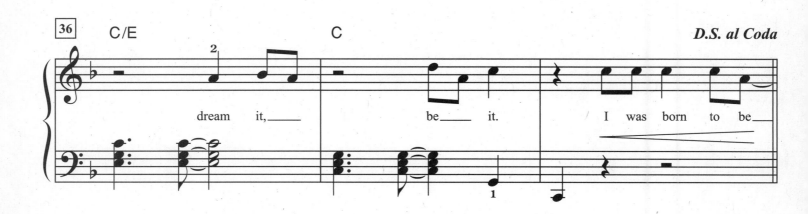

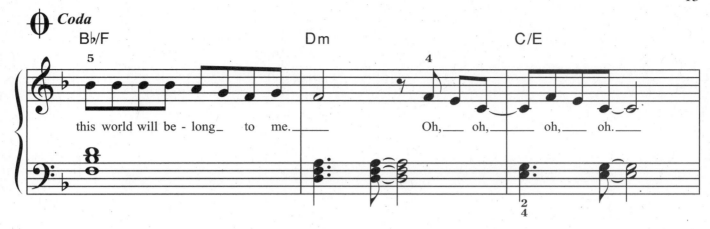

Verse 2:
This life can kick you around.
This world can make you feel small.
But they will not keep me down.
I was born to stand tall.
I'm going all the way.
I can feel it, I believe it.
I'm here, I'm here to stay.
(To Chorus:)

DREAM IS COLLAPSING

(from *Inception*)

Composed by Hans Zimmer
Arranged by Dan Coates

FIREWORK

Words and Music by
Katy Perry, Mikkel Eriksen, Tor Erik Hermansen,
Sandy Wilhelm and Ester Dean
Arranged by Dan Coates

Moderately, with a steady beat

𝄋 *Chorus:*

of Ju - ly. 'Cause ba-by, you're a fi - re-work.

Come on, show 'em what you're worth. Make 'em go

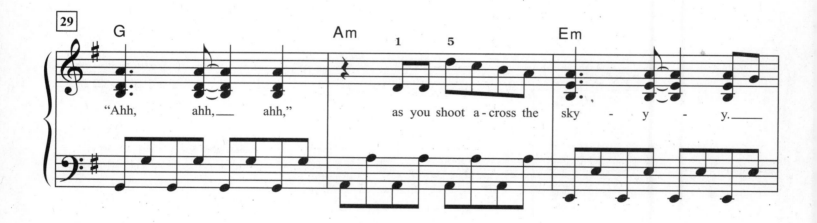

"Ahh, ahh, ahh," as you shoot a-cross the sky - y - y.

Ba-by, you're a fi - re-work. Come on, let your

Coda

And now, it's time to let it through. 'Cause ba - by, you're a

awe, awe, awe.

Boom, boom, boom, e - ven bright-er than the moon, moon, moon.

FORGET YOU

Words and Music by
Christopher Brown, Peter Hernandez, Ari Levine,
Philip Lawrence and Thomas "Cee Lo" Callaway
Arranged by Dan Coates

Moderately fast

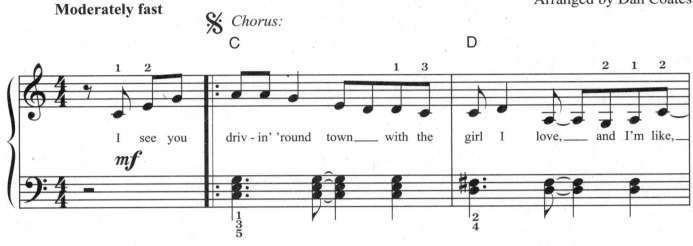

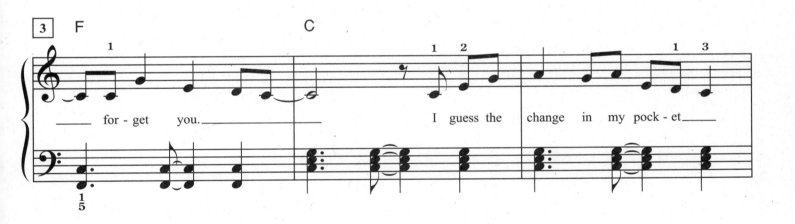

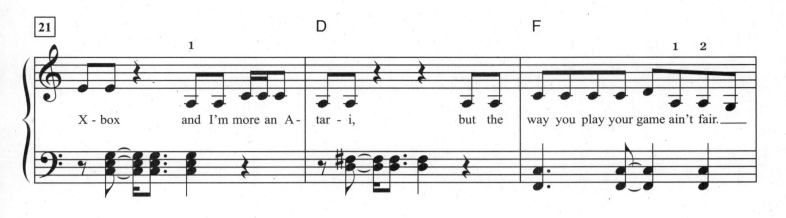

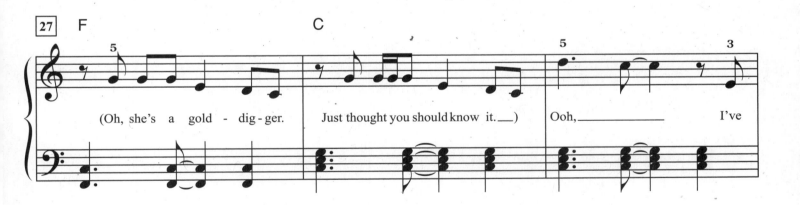

28

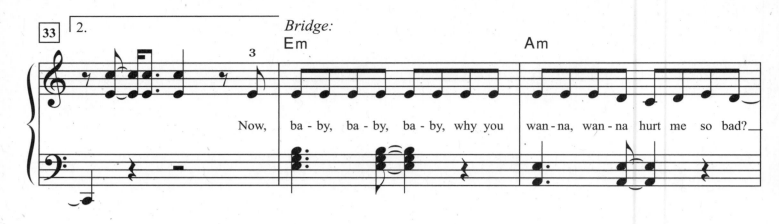

la - dy?_____   I love you,   I still love_____

you._____   I see you

Verse 2:
Now, I know that I had to borrow,
Beg and steal and lie and cheat,
Tryin' to keep ya, tryin' to please ya,
'Cause being in love with your a** ain't cheap.

GRENADE

Words and Music by
Claude Kelly, Peter Hernandez, Brody Brown,
Philip Lawrence, Ari Levine and Andrew Wyatt
Arranged by Dan Coates

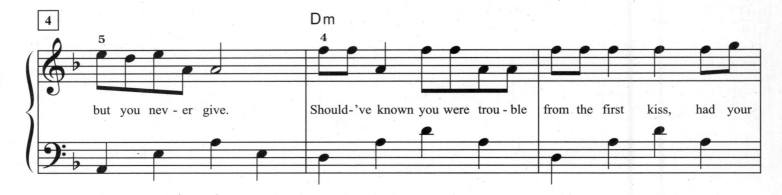

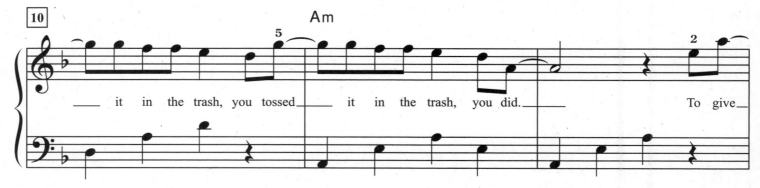

go through all___ this pain,___ take a bul - let straight through___ my brain.

___ Yes, I would die___ for you ba - by, but you won't do the same.

but you won't do the same.

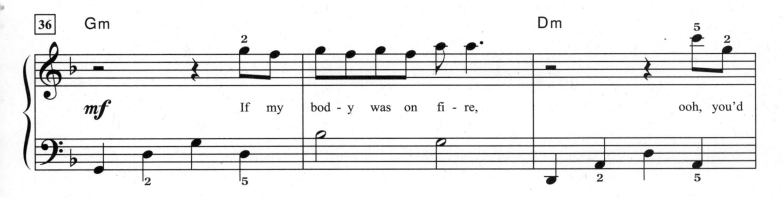

D.S. al Coda

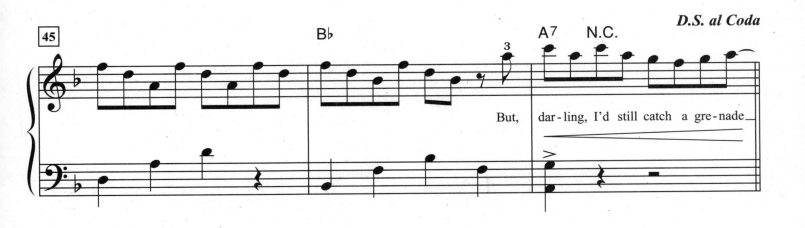

Verse 2:
Black, black, black and blue, beat me 'til I'm numb.
Tell the devil I said "Hey" when you get back to where you're from.
Mad woman, bad woman, that's just what you are.
Yeah, you'll smile in my face then rip the brakes out my car.
Gave you all I had and you tossed it in the trash,
You tossed it in the trash, you did.
To give me all your love is all I ever asked.
'Cause what you don't understand is I'd catch a grenade for you...
(To Chorus:)

HAVEN'T MET YOU YET

Words and Music by
Michael Bublé, Alan Chang and Amy Foster
Arranged by Dan Coates

so we can work to work it out. And I pro - mise you, kid,____ that I'll give

____ so much more____ than I get.____ I just have - n't met you

dim.

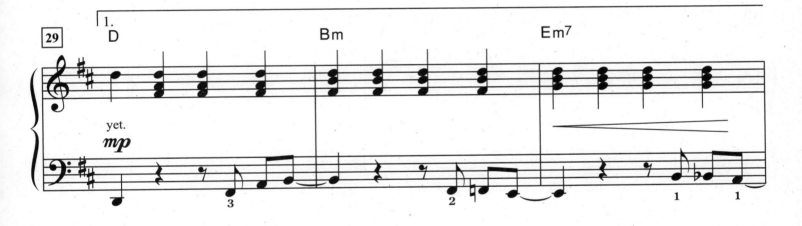

yet.

mp

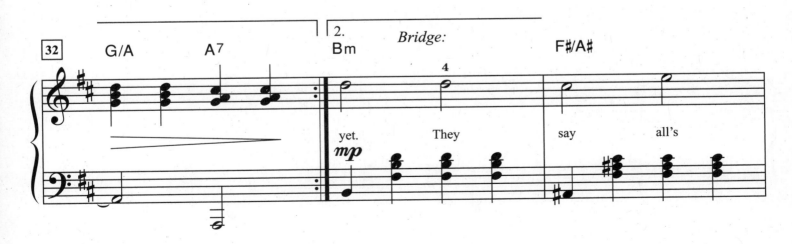

yet. They say all's

mp

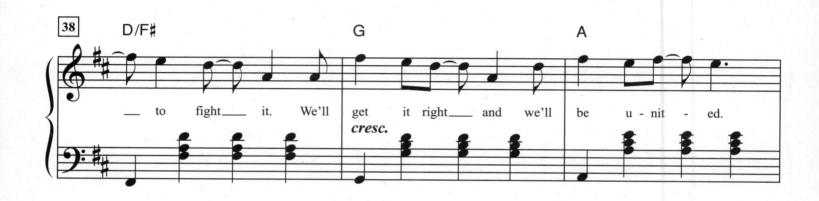

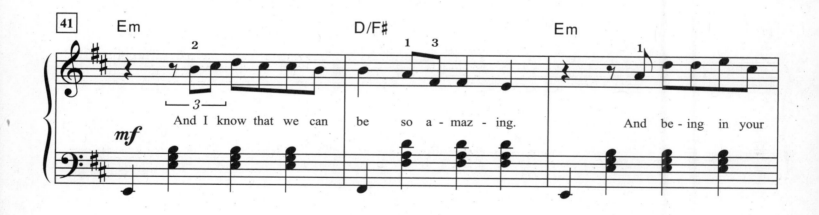

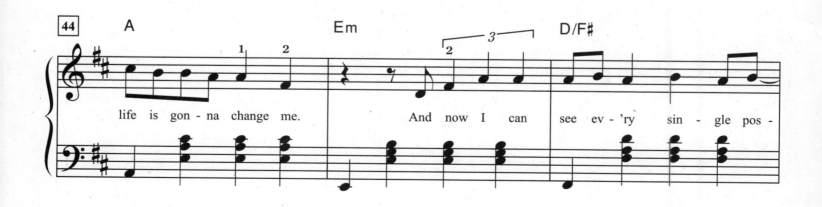

JAR OF HEARTS

Words and Music by
Drew Lawrence, Christina Perri and Barrett Yeretsian
Arranged by Dan Coates

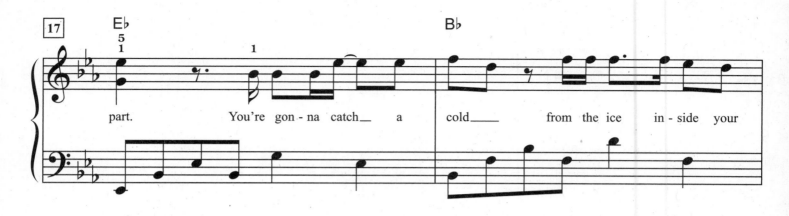

17 E♭ ... B♭

part. You're gon - na catch___ a cold___ from the ice in - side your

19 Cm ... *to Coda* ⊕ A♭ ... A♭m

soul,_____ so don't come back for me. Who do you think you

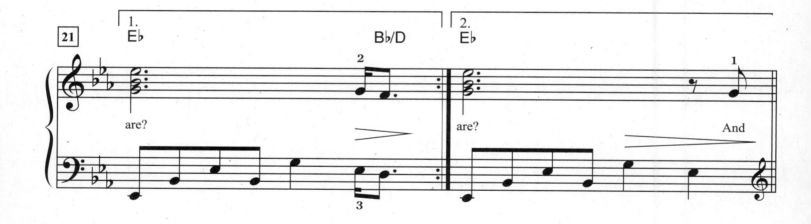

21 1. E♭ ... B♭/D | 2. E♭

are? | are? And

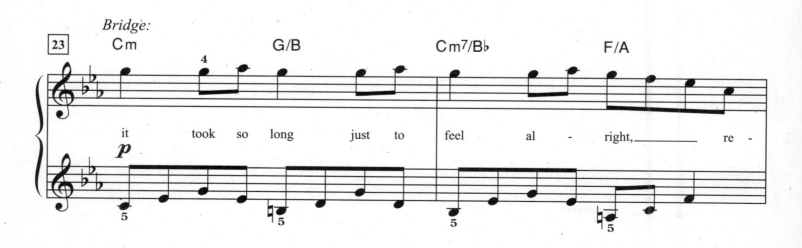

Bridge:

23 Cm ... G/B ... Cm7/B♭ ... F/A

it took so long just to feel al - right,_____ re -

p

Verse 2:
I hear you're asking all around
If I am anywhere to be found.
But I have grown too strong
To ever fall back in your arms.
And I learned to live half alive,
And now you want me one more time.
(To Chorus:)

NOT LIKE THE MOVIES

Words and Music by
Katy Perry and Greg Wells
Arranged by Dan Coates

Verse 2:
Snow White said when I was young,
"One day my prince will come."
So I wait for that date.
They say it's hard to meet your match,
Gotta find my better half,
So we make perfect shapes.
If stars don't align, if it doesn't stop time,
If you can't see the sign, wait for it.
One hundred percent, worth every penny spent,
He'll be the one that finishes your sentences.
(To Chorus:)

JUST THE WAY YOU ARE (AMAZING)

Words and Music by
Khalil Walton, Peter Hernandez,
Philip Lawrence, Ari Levine and Khari Cain
Arranged by Dan Coates

13 B♭ ... F

She's so beau - ti - ful, and I tell her ev - 'ry - day. _____

16

Yeah, *mf* I know,___ I know___ when I com-pli-ment___ her, she won't be-lieve me.

19 Dm7 ... B♭

And it's so,___ it's so___ sad to think that she don't see what I see. But ev - 'ry time she asks me,

22 ... F

"Do I look o - kay?"___ I say... When I see your face,___

Chorus:

there's not a thing ___ that I ___ would change,

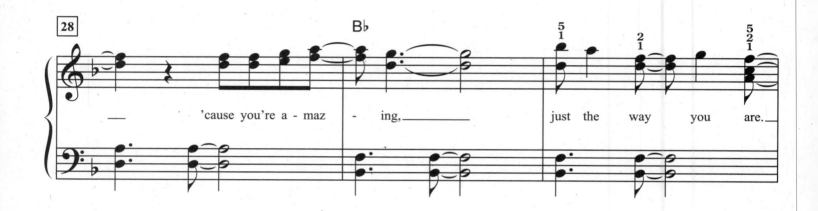

___ 'cause you're a - maz - ing, _____ just the way you are.

___ And when you smile, ___

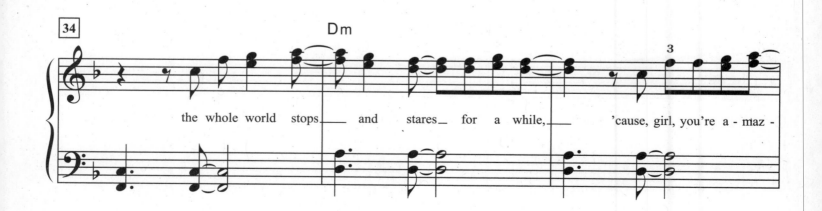

the whole world stops ___ and stares ___ for a while, ___ 'cause, girl, you're a - maz -

Verse 2:
Her lips, her lips, I could kiss them all day if she'd let me.
Her laugh, her laugh, she hates, but I think it's so sexy.
She's so beautiful and I tell her every day.
Oh, you know, you know, you know I'd never ask you to change.
If perfect's what you're searching for, then just stay the same.
So don't even bother asking if you look okay. You know I'll say...
(To Chorus:)

YOU HAVEN'T SEEN THE LAST OF ME

(from *Burlesque*)

Words and Music by Diane Warren
Arranged by Dan Coates

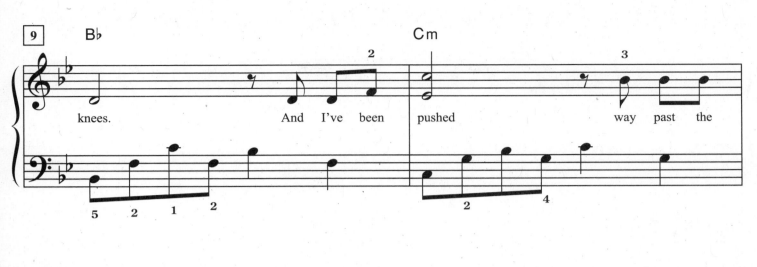

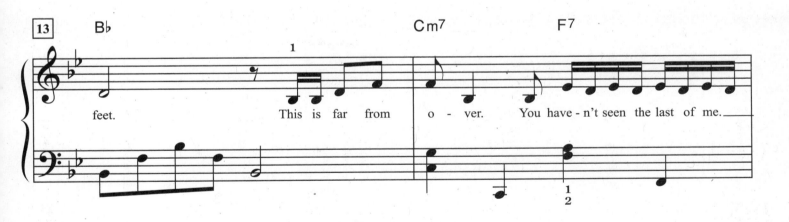

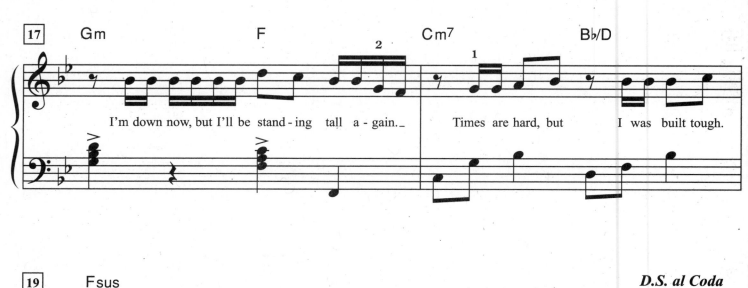

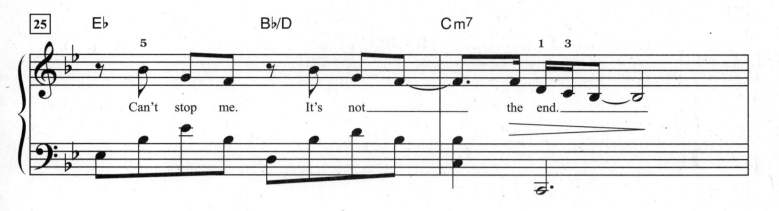

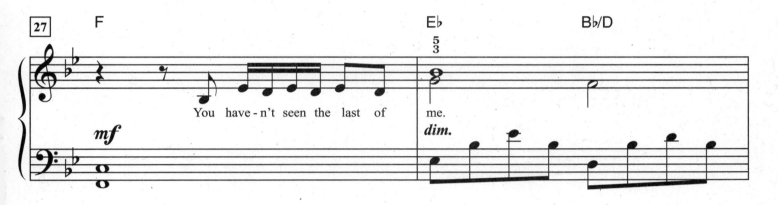

Verse 2:
They can say that I won't stay around,
But I'm gonna stand my ground.
You're not gonna stop me.
You don't know me, you don't know who I am.
Don't count me out so fast.
(To Chorus:)

OBLIVIATE

(from *Harry Potter and The Deathly Hallows, Part 1*)

By Alexandre Desplat
Arranged by Dan Coates

Moderately slow (♩ = 76)